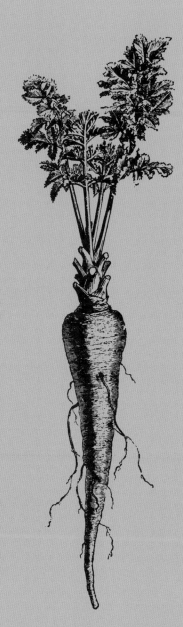

Rosehips
on a
Kitchen Table

SEASONAL RECIPES FOR FORAGERS & FOODIES

CAROLYN CALDICOTT

PHOTOGRAPHS BY CHRIS CALDICOTT
FOOD STYLING BY CAROLYN CALDICOTT

F

FRANCES LINCOLN LIMITED
PUBLISHERS

Frances Lincoln Limited
74–77 White Lion Street
London N1 9PF
www.franceslincoln.com

A catalogue record for this book is available
from the British Library.

978-0-7112-3388-1

9 8 7 6 5 4 3 2 1

Contents

Rich Pickings

You don't have to be an expert cook, gardener or forager to make the most of this book – you just have to love good seasonal food.

In *Rosehips on a Kitchen Table* we show you how you can use old-fashioned methods – with a contemporary twist – to turn gluts, wild pickings and long-neglected ingredients into quick lunches, inventive suppers and divine desserts. Maybe we can even tempt you to dabble in the world of grow your own. Convert the gnarled and knobbly, weird and wonderful, into jams and jellies, chutneys, pickles, pesto and cordials. Plunge in with an open mind and get cooking!

Useful things to know

- A few phrases that pop up a lot are 'blanch', 'setting point', 'sterilize' and 'seal'.
  - To blanch vegetables, bring a pan of water to a brisk boil, dunk the prepared vegetables in the water, drain, then refresh with cold water.
  - The setting point is the point at which a jam or jelly will set once cooled. To test, spoon a teaspoon of the jam or jelly on to a cold saucer. Leave it for a minute or two to cool, then push it with your finger. If the surface wrinkles the jam's ready to set. If it's still runny, boil for a little longer and test again.
  - I find that the easiest way to sterilize jars and bottles is first to wash the jars and lids in hot, soapy water, then place them in an oven and set the oven temperature to 100°C/200°F. When the oven is up to temperature the jars and lids are ready to use.
  - To store jam or jelly, ladle the fruit mixture into sterilized jars as soon as the setting point is reached. Cover the jam with a waxed jam disc (waxed side down). You can then either seal with a tight-fitting lid or use a cellophane jam cover: moisten the cellophane with a drop of water, stretch over the jar (damp side up) and secure with a rubber band. (Whichever way you choose, the jars will look very pretty covered with fabric or coloured paper – available from good cooks' shops, or make your own.) Syrups are best stored in sterilized screw-top bottles. Store chutneys and vinegars in jars with plastic-lined lids or in Kilner jars or bottles with rubber-sealed clips.
- Don't discard old jars and bottles; you never know when they'll come in handy.
- Have a selection of labels to hand: you don't want to get your dates mixed up.
- A hand-operated mouli is a useful tool to invest in. It makes light of any sieving job. Maybe you even have one lurking in the back of a cupboard?
- A jelly bag is a fine mesh fabric bag especially designed to strain fruit. To scald the bag, iron both sides with an iron heated to a medium temperature or immerse in boiling water for a few minutes.
- Wash all vegetables and fruit thoroughly before use.
- When using the recipes in this book, please follow either metric or American measurements. Don't mix the two – they are not exact equivalents.
- Recipes are for 4 greedy or 6 moderate people, unless otherwise stated.

Gleaning

*T*here's nothing quite as satisfying as foraging for free wild food. A handful of nettles for a warming soup, some wild garlic to whizz with olive oil to make a simple pesto, rosehips for a jelly packed with vitamin C? It's all out there for the picking, even in the city, as long as you know what to look for.

Keep your eyes open and always be prepared with a handy spare bag in your pocket. A stout walking stick can also be very useful to hook a stray branch; you can bet the biggest and best produce is just out of arm's reach.

Whether in the town or the country, stick to a few basic rules; pick produce well away from the path or road; if there's only a small amount leave it to grow; never dig up a plant; and, most important, if in doubt don't pick it! Once at home with your bounty make sure to wash everything thoroughly before you eat it.

Once you've been bitten by the foraging bug you'll be amazed how much wild produce there is around. As the seasons progress new treats constantly reveal themselves. Blackberries climbing over a park fence, a rogue apple or damson tree; another one for the list. All my secret locations are carefully documented in a treasured battered notebook as a reminder for next year. So get out there and get picking: the rewards are huge.

Wild Garlic

In early spring, when snowdrops raise their nodding heads, the first optimistic shoots of wild garlic push through the earth. As the days start to warm, the shoots erupt into a bright green carpet of long, pointed leaves, garlanded with delicate white flowers.

A member of the *Allium* family, wild garlic, or ramson, flourishes in moist wooded areas and is instantly recognizable by – the strong smell of garlic! Once picked the leaves keep well when stored in the fridge, so don't be shy about how much you take. Remember to pick a posy of the edible white flowers: they make a tasty, pretty garnish for any wild garlic recipe.

After the long winter months wild garlic makes a welcome leafy green addition to the plate; it can be used as a herb or like spinach. Add to soups and bakes, tear into salads or blend to make a robust pesto. For a quick supper stuff chicken breasts with finely sliced leaves and fry in olive oil until golden; or simply blanch handfuls in boiling water and toss in the juices of a Sunday roast. (Just remember that wild garlic wilts considerably when simmered in boiling water.)

Wild garlic can be preserved using the same method as nettles (see page 18).

WILD GARLIC PESTO

Perk up pasta with a blast of flavour! Serve with your favourite pasta topped with grated Parmesan cheese or spoon on to soups, baked potatoes or risotto. Pesto stores well in the fridge: just make sure there is always a layer of olive oil on top to seal the pesto from the air. This recipe can also be made with young nettle leaves; add a plump clove of chopped garlic to the ingredients before blending.

2 good handfuls of washed wild garlic leaves
a handful of pine nuts, chopped walnuts or pumpkin seeds
110ml/½ cup extra virgin olive oil
a squeeze of lemon juice
a little fresh chilli (optional)
salt and black pepper to taste

Plunge the wild garlic leaves into rapidly boiling water, drain and refresh with cold water. Squeeze any excess water away and blend with the remaining ingredients until finely chopped. Scoop into a sterilized jar, pour a thin layer of olive oil on top and seal with a tight-fitting lid. Store in the fridge until ready to use.

WILD GARLIC BROTH

A clear, delicately scented broth topped with wild garlic flowers. Add the wild garlic just before serving, to preserve the flavour and bright green colour of the leaves.

3 young leeks, topped and tailed, washed and thinly sliced
salt and black pepper
2 good-sized handfuls of wild garlic leaves, washed and thinly sliced
wild garlic flowers to garnish

For the broth
1.5 litres/6 cups good chicken or vegetable stock
1 leek, topped and tailed, cleaned and cut into big chunks
1 medium onion, peeled and quartered
2 carrots, peeled and cut in half
2 celery sticks, cut into large chunks
1 teaspoon black peppercorns
2 bay leaves
1 plump clove of garlic

First make the broth. Pour the stock into a saucepan, add the vegetables, pepper, bay leaves and garlic, cover the pan and gently simmer for 20 minutes.

Strain the broth into a large bowl and return the resulting liquid to the pan. Add the sliced young leeks and seasoning to taste. Cover the pan and simmer until the leeks are soft.

Add the sliced wild garlic. After a few minutes, when the leaves have wilted, the soup is ready to serve. Ladle into bowls and carefully float wild garlic flowers on top.

WILD GARLIC DAUPHINOISE

A forager's twist on the classic creamy sliced potato bake. The trick to a good dauphinoise is to cut the potatoes as thin as you dare.

4 largish waxy potatoes, peeled and thinly sliced
1 medium onion, thinly sliced
a large handful of wild garlic, well washed and thinly sliced
300ml/1¼ cups double cream
150ml/⅔ cup good vegetable stock
nutmeg
a small bunch of thyme
salt and black pepper
butter

Preheat the oven to 190°C/375°F/gas mark 5.

Butter a baking dish and line with a layer of sliced potatoes. Sprinkle with a little sliced onion, wild garlic, a good grating of nutmeg, thyme, salt and freshly ground black pepper. Continue to layer the potatoes in this way until all the ingredients have been used up, making sure to finish with a layer of potato.

Pour the stock and cream evenly over the top and dot with the butter. Cover with kitchen foil and bake in the oven for 45 minutes. Remove the foil, turn the oven up to 200°C/400F°/gas mark 6 and bake for a further 20 minutes, until the dauphinoise is brown and crispy on top.

Nettles

Nettles are everywhere. They just are. The ultimate free superfood packed full of protein, iron, magnesium and vitamins A, C, D and B complex. Their pleasing earthy flavour is making its way on to some of the most fashionable menus.

Nettles are at their best in the spring when the plants are small and the leaves tender; by the summer months they have become too fibrous to eat. Wade into battle armed with a protective gauntlet of rubber gloves and long trousers tucked into wellies. Gather leaves well away from the path, selecting the new growth at the top of the plant: as a basic rule I tend to collect the top four leaves.

Nettles are remarkably versatile. Nettle soup makes a simple nutritious lunch and risotto an adventurous supper. Add a handful of blanched leaves to an omelette batter or ward off hay fever with antihistamine-rich nettle tea; brew a handful of nettle leaves in boiling water for 5 minutes. Dollop nettle pesto on to new potatoes: simply follow the recipe for wild garlic pesto (see page 13), substituting nettle leaves for the wild garlic and adding a plump chopped garlic clove to the mixture before blending.

If you enjoy the taste, prolong the pleasure: blanch washed nettle leaves, finely chop in a food processor and freeze in portions in an ice cube tray. When the cubes are frozen, remove from the tray and store in a sealed plastic bag. Alternatively, blend blanched leaves with oil and store in sterilized jars in the fridge: just make sure the puréed nettles are covered with a layer of oil.

NETTLE SOUP

A thick, comforting soup for a spring day.
This recipe also works well with wild garlic leaves.

3 rubber-gloved large handfuls of
  young nettle leaves
a large handful of spinach leaves
olive oil
1 medium onion, finely chopped
3 cloves of garlic, finely chopped
3 medium potatoes, peeled and
  cubed

3 celery sticks, sliced
1.5 litres/6 cups vegetable or
  chicken stock
nutmeg
salt and black pepper
double cream
chives, to garnish

Thoroughly wash the nettle leaves, wearing rubber gloves. Destalk and slice the spinach leaves.

Cover the bottom of a medium-sized saucepan with olive oil. When hot add the chopped onion and garlic and sauté until translucent. Add the potato and celery and cook until the potato starts to soften.

Pour in the stock, cover the pan and gently simmer until the potatoes are soft.

Add rubber-gloved handfuls of nettles and sliced spinach to the pan. Simmer for a few minutes longer. When the leaves begin to wilt remove the pan from the heat immediately. Take care not to overcook the leaves at this stage or the soup will lose its bright green colour.

Add a good grating of nutmeg and season to taste. Liquidize the soup until thick and smooth.

Serve topped with a swirl of double cream and chopped chives.

NETTLE RISOTTO

It's stunning how good this bright green risotto tastes.
Nettles and risotto rice are simply made for each other.

3 rubber-gloved large handfuls of
washed young nettle leaves
3 tablespoons butter
1 tablespoon olive oil
1 small red onion, diced
2 young leeks, cleaned and thinly sliced
400g/2 cups arborio rice
110ml/½ cup dry white wine
1 litre/4 cups hot chicken or
vegetable stock

75g/1 cup grated Parmesan cheese
a handful of chopped parsley
a knob of butter
salt and black pepper

To garnish
rocket leaves
extra grated Parmesan
a drizzle of olive oil

Drop the nettle leaves into a pan of rapidly boiling water. After no longer than a minute, drain the nettles and refresh with cold water. Blend the leaves in a processor until finely chopped.

In a heavy-bottomed pan, heat the butter and the olive oil. When the butter has melted, add the diced onion and leeks and sauté until soft, but not brown.

Stir in the arborio rice until coated with butter, pour in the white wine and stir until the wine has been absorbed.

Gradually add the hot stock, a ladle at a time, making sure all the stock has been absorbed before adding the next ladle. Stir continually to achieve the perfect creamy risotto.

Add the prepared nettles, grated Parmesan, parsley, a large knob of butter and seasoning to taste. Stir until well combined.

Serve topped with rocket leaves, extra grated Parmesan and a drizzle of olive oil.

Elderflowers and elderberries

Elder bushes are prolific in hedgerows, parkland and embankments. In late spring, as the days start to lengthen, elderflowers burst into bloom, a profusion of creamy white flower heads. Time to get picking – the season is short.

Gather flower heads early in the season, when the tiny star-shaped flowers are open but not dropping. Give the heads a good shake to remove any insects before you add them to your bag.

The heady floral scent of elderflowers adds a delicate flavour to puddings and preserves. The flowers can be tied in muslin and simmered directly with ingredients, or added as a cordial. Cordial preserves the subtle flavour of elderflowers until well after the last flowers have withered. Add it to custards and tarts, milky panna cotta, poached pears, fools and jellies, or dilute with water for a delicious drink.

Don't forget the copious clusters of deep purple berries rich in vitamin C that follow the elderflowers in late summer. Add them to jams, pies and puds or whizz cooked elderberries in a blender with a little sugar to make a delicious – and eye-catching – fruit coulis. Elderberry cordial, a traditional cure for colds, is very simple to prepare: cover washed berries with water and simmer until soft; sieve the fruit and for every 600ml/2½ cups of liquid collected add 400g/2 cups of sugar, 6 cloves and the juice of a lemon. Briskly simmer for a further 10 minutes and decant into sterilized bottles.

The quickest way to remove the berries from the stalk is to run the stalk through the prongs of a fork. Once picked the berries have a short shelf life: store in the fridge or freeze whole until ready to use.

ELDERFLOWER AND LIME CORDIAL

Light and fragrant, elderflower cordial diluted with sparkling water makes a
thirst-quenching summer drink. if you prefer something a little stronger,
mix the cordial with vodka, soda, a squeeze of lime juice and a sprig of mint.
To decorate and cool your glass, freeze tiny elderflowers in ice cubes.
Stored in the fridge the cordial will keep for six weeks or so. For a longer
shelf life freeze it in ice cube trays; place the frozen cubes in sealed plastic bags.

MAKES ABOUT 1.5 LITRES/6 CUPS

20 elderflower heads
3 limes
1.5 litres/6 cups water
800g/4 cups caster sugar

Pick flowers that are open but not dropping. Cut the stem off with a pair of
scissors, wash the flowers and place in a large saucepan.

Squeeze the limes, add the skins to the saucepan and set the juice to one side.
Add the water to the pan, cover and bring to the boil. Reduce the heat and gently
simmer for 10 minutes. Remove the pan from the heat and leave to stand for half
an hour.

Strain the liquid through a scalded jelly bag or muslin-lined sieve into a clean
saucepan. Add the caster sugar and lime juice and stir over a low heat until the
sugar has dissolved. Turn up the heat and fast boil for 5 minutes.

Decant into sterilized bottles while still hot; seal immediately.

ELDERFLOWER GRANITA

To make this refreshing icy treat, dilute 1 part elderflower cordial to 2 parts still mineral water in a freezer-proof tub. Add lime juice and zest to taste, cover the tub and place in the freezer. After 2 hours stir with a fork to break up any crystals of ice that have formed. Return the tub to the freezer. Repeat the stirring process 2 or 3 more times, until the granita has the consistency of crushed ice, then leave to freeze completely. To serve, allow the granita to defost a little, then pour into glasses and add a dash of vodka, some fresh mint leaves and a few freshly picked elderflowers.

ELDERBERRY SUMMER PUDDING

For this quintessentially English pudding – with a difference –
combine elderberries with other seasonal berries and currants.
To complete the experience, smother with double cream.
The fruit compote in this recipe can also be layered with trifle sponges,
custard and whipped cream to create a good old-fashioned trifle.
You will need a medium-sized pudding bowl.

200g/7oz prepared elderberries
350g/12oz raspberries
175g/6oz blackberries
175g/6oz redcurrants
(or mixed berries and currants of your choice)
2 tablespoons water
caster sugar
8 medium-cut slices white bread (large loaf size)

Place the berries in a saucepan with the water and caster sugar to taste. Gently simmer for a few minutes until the sugar dissolves and the berries split to release their juice. Take care not to overcook the fruit.

Cut the crusts from the bread and line the pudding basin. Start by placing a slice of bread in the bottom of the bowl, then position overlapping slices around the edge. Fill any holes with smaller pieces of bread – there must be no gaps. Keep some bread aside to top the pudding.

Spoon the fruit into the bread-lined basin, reserving a few tablespoons of juice for later. Cover the fruit with overlapping bread slices. Place a saucer small enough to fit inside the bowl on top of the pudding and put a heavy weight on top of the saucer: this is essential to compact the pudding and push the juices into the bread. Keep the pudding in the fridge overnight to give the alchemy time to work.

Remove the weight and saucer just before serving. Run a palette knife around the edge, place a large plate over the top of the bowl and carefully turn the pudding out on to the plate. Use the reserved juice to cover any bits of bread that are not completely soaked. Don't worry if it collapses a little!

HEDGEROW JAM

A combination of elderberries and blackberries makes a superb dark purple jam (you can also throw in peeled, cored, diced apple if you have a glut).

For every 450g/1lb fruit you will need 350g/1¾ cups granulated sugar and the juice of a lemon.

Simmer the fruit with a little water (just enough to stop the fruit sticking), until it starts to break down. Add the sugar and lemon juice and stir over a low heat until all the sugar has dissolved. Turn up the heat and boil briskly until the setting point is reached (see page 9). Ladle the hot jam into sterilized jars, cover with waxed jam discs and seal immediately.

Blackberries

Childhood memories of purple-stained fingers, snagged cardigans and scratched arms always flood back when I am picking blackberries. My lovely mother was an enthusiastic gatherer of blackberries and late summer family outings were always a thinly disguised opportunity to get us all helping with the task. We were easily bribed with the promise of a picnic lunch and the rewards were always worth the effort. Crumbles and pies, jams, jellies and fruit cheese soon filled the table.

Picking blackberries is now, for me, a labour of love. Thankfully, these scented, sweet and juicy, deep purple fruits are hard to miss. Their arched stems vigorously tangle through hedgerows, woodlands, wasteland, parks and ditches. Filled to the brim with vitamins, folic acid and antioxidants, blackberries have supplemented our diet for thousands of years. Add a handful to porridge or muesli or purée and serve with yoghurt.

Harvest the blackberries when they are plump and soft but do not collapse to the touch (it is best to use a solid-bottomed tub or basket as blackberries crush under their own weight). Keep in mind that the berries growing in full sun are usually the sweetest. Creepy-crawlies love blackberries, so make sure to soak the berries in water for half an hour before thoroughly rinsing. Store washed berries in the fridge or freeze until you are ready to use them.

BLACKBERRY VINEGAR

Any surplus blackberries can be used to make blackberry vinegar. Mix into salad dressings, sprinkle on strawberries or add a dash to a cup of hot water and honey for an age-old cold remedy.

MAKES ABOUT 600ML/2½ CUPS

450g/1lb washed blackberries
2 tablespoons golden caster sugar
600ml/2½ cups red wine vinegar

Place the blackberries in a sterilized Kilner jar, sprinkle with the caster sugar and top with the vinegar. Seal the jar and store in a dark place for 4 weeks, rolling the jar a couple of times to help the sugar dissolve. Strain the vinegar, pour into sterilized bottles and seal immediately.

BLACKBERRY AND RARE ROAST BEEF SALAD

Blackberries are particularly good with beef, game or lamb. This recipe is an excellent way to use up any leftovers from a Sunday roast.

blackberry vinegar
olive oil
walnut oil
grainy mustard
salt and black pepper
blackberries (around 10 per person)
port
rocket and watercress
thickly sliced rare roast beef
chopped walnuts

Whisk one-third part blackberry vinegar, one-third part olive oil and one-third part walnut oil with a little grainy mustard. Season to taste.

Poach the blackberries for a couple of minutes in a splash of port. Remove the blackberries with a slotted spoon and set to one side. Add the remaining port to the dressing.

Top spicy rocket and watercress leaves with thick slices of rare roast beef. Sprinkle with the chopped walnuts and poached blackberries and drizzle with the dressing.

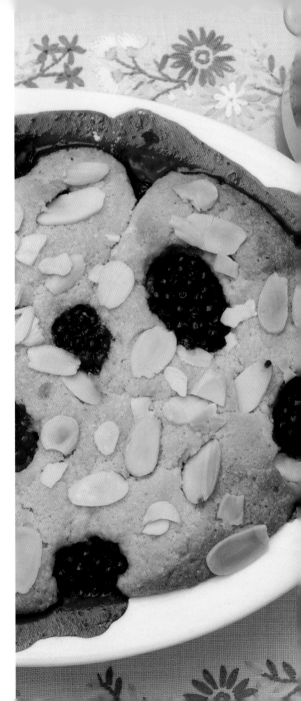

BLACKBERRY AND APPLE ALMOND-CRUSTED PUDDING

My favourite childhood pudding. I still treasure the original juice-splattered recipe written in my mother's sloping handwriting. These days I have less of a sweet tooth and tend not to sweeten the fruit, but you can add sugar to taste. Serve with lashings of thick custard.

For the fruit filling
350g/12oz washed blackberries
450g/1lb sweet apples
1 teaspoon vanilla extract
golden caster sugar

For the almond crust
75g/½ cup self-raising flour
75g/¾ cup ground almonds
50g/¼ cup soft brown sugar
50g/½ stick soft butter
110ml/½ cup single cream or whole milk
a handful of flaked almonds

Preheat the oven to 190C°/375°F/gas mark 5 and butter a deep pie dish.

Check the blackberries to make sure there are no stalks still attached.

Peel and core the apples, cut into chunks and simmer with a splash of water (just enough to stop the apples sticking) until they are soft but not breaking down. Add the vanilla extract, sugar to taste and blackberries. Cook for a couple of minutes, until the juice starts to run from the blackberries. Spoon the mixture into the prepared pie dish.

Mix the flour, ground almonds and sugar together. Cut the butter into small pieces, add to the flour mixture and rub in until breadcrumbs form. Pour in the single cream and combine together to make a stiff mixture.

Spoon dollops of the mixture on to the cooked fruit, to give a cobbled effect. Sprinkle with flaked almonds.

Place the pudding on a baking tray and bake in the preheated oven for 30 minutes until golden brown.

Rosehips

During the autumn months rosy red rosehips, the bountiful fruit of the pale pink wild rose, whose thorny branches clamber unchecked through our hedgerows, are ripe and ready to pick. Rich in vitamin C and antioxidants, rosehips are just too good to pass by.

Pick preferably after the first frost, when the rosehips are soft to the touch but not squidgy. Watch out for the bushes' snagging thorns and don't be tempted to taste the hips whole: rosehips contain hairy seeds that are used in the manufacture of itching powder. Use scissors to top and tail the rosehips, and remember to cook them in a stainless steel or enamel pan (they would corrode a reactive pan).

Moreish rosehip syrup is famous for keeping colds at bay. Rosehips also make a good tangy fruity jelly and a vitamin C boosting tea; roughly chop a small handful of hips and infuse in hot water for 5 minutes before sweetening with a spoonful of runny honey.

ROSEHIP SYRUP

Rosehip syrup doesn't have to be limited to medicinal uses. You can pour it over ice cream or pancakes, add it to a stiff vodka and tonic or mix with sparkling water for a tart teetotal cordial. Store the syrup in sterilized screw-top bottles. I recommend using smallish bottles as the syrup has a short shelf life once the bottle is opened.

MAKES ABOUT 1.5 LITRES/6 CUPS

900g/2lb washed rosehips
2.25 litres/9 cups water
450g/2¼ cups white granulated sugar
jelly bag or muslin square

Top and tail the rosehips and roughly chop in a food processor.

Bring about 1.5 litres/6 cups of the water to the boil, add the chopped rosehips and bring back to the boil. Remove the pan from the heat, cover and leave to stand for half an hour.

Strain the mixture through a scalded jelly bag or muslin-lined plastic sieve. Squeeze the bag to remove all the liquid and set to one side.

Return the pulp to the pan with the remaining water, bring to the boil, remove from the heat, cover and set aside for a further half hour. Strain once more.

Combine the strained liquids in a clean pan, add the sugar and stir over a low heat until dissolved. Simmer the liquid until it has a syrupy cordial consistency.

Decant into sterilized bottles and screw down the tops immediately.

ROSEHIP AND APPLE JELLY

A beautiful clear fruit jelly, perfect to spread on hot buttered toast,
or serve with cheese or a Sunday roast.
Rosehips are low in pectin, so it is a good idea to add apples to aid the set of the
jelly. Roughly chop the whole apple (the skin and core contain valuable pectin);
if you have a supply of crab apples or quince even better.
To make blackberry jelly, replace the rosehips with the same weight of berries.

MAKES ABOUT 3 x 450G/1LB JARS

450g/1lb rosehips
900g/2lb apples, crab apples or quince
zest and juice of a lemon
jam sugar

Wash the rosehips and apples. Roughly chop the rosehips in a food processor and quarter the apples. Place in a stainless steel pan and add the lemon zest and juice and enough water to just cover the fruit. Cover the pan and simmer until the apples are really soft. Remove from the heat and allow to stand for 20 minutes.

Strain the liquid through a scalded jelly bag or a muslin-lined sieve placed over a large, deep bowl. Ideally, leave the mixture overnight to ensure all the extracted liquid has drained from the pulp. Resist any temptation to squeeze the bag – if you do this you'll get a cloudy jelly.

Measure the extracted liquid and, based on the proportions of 450g/2¼ cups jam sugar to 600ml/2½ cups juice, measure the quantity of sugar required. Combine the liquid and sugar in a stainless steel pan and stir over a low heat until the sugar has dissolved. Bring to boiling point and briskly simmer for 15 minutes or so, until the setting point is reached (see page 9).

Ladle into sterilized jars, cover with a waxed jam disc and seal immediately with a tight-fitting lid.

Sloes

Whiling away a winter's afternoon at the local pub's annual sloe gin competition was not only a lot of fun, but also the perfect opportunity to seek out the judges' criteria for a prize-winning sloe gin. Chatting with fellow contestants over a pint proved to be an invaluable source of information as well. Treasured recipes, handed down through generations, were swapped and hastily scribbled on the back of beer mats. By the end of the day third prize for the best sloe gin was proudly sitting on my mantelpiece. With all my gleaned tips, hopefully it will be joined by first prize next year.

If you are not familiar with sloes, they are the plump deep purple fruit of the blackthorn tree, a little similar in appearance to a blueberry. The similarity ends there: unlike blueberries, raw sloes have a bitter astringent taste and a hard central stone. But over the centuries such an abundant hedgerow crop proved too valuable to ignore: the result of our ancestors' experiments is a plethora of recipes transforming the bitter sloe into a delicious treat.

Gather sloes in the autumn when they are ripe and soft to the touch, taking care to avoid the trees' sharp long thorns. The traditional advice is to wait until after the first frost, which sweetens the fruit. But wait too long at your peril: birds love sloes. And popping the harvested fruit in the freezer has the same sweetening effect.

TIPSY SLOE FAIRY CAKES

Dainty fairy cakes with a hidden tipsy heart.

MAKES 12

110g/1 stick soft butter
100g/½ cup caster sugar
2 medium free-range eggs
1 teaspoon vanilla extract
110g/¾ cup self-raising flour
puréed gin-soaked sloes

To serve
icing sugar and crème fraîche or clotted cream

Preheat the oven to 180°C/350°F/gas mark 4.

Prepare your cake tray by placing 12 paper cake cases in the indents of a 12-hole tart tray.

Cream the butter and caster sugar together until the mixture is very light and fluffy.

Beat in each egg one at a time.

Beat in the vanilla extract.

Carefully fold in the flour until all is well combined.

Two-thirds fill the prepared cases with cake mixture. Make a small indent in the top of each one and spoon in ½ teaspoon of the sloe gin purée.

Bake on the middle shelf of the oven for 15–18 minutes, until golden brown. The cake should spring back when lightly pressed in the middle.

Dust with icing sugar and serve with crème fraîche or clotted cream.

Grow Your Own

*M*y attitude to venturing into the world of grow your own is to keep it simple. I go mostly for produce that is difficult or expensive to buy, but reasonably easy to grow. The plants have to be tolerant of pests, poor soil and challenging weather and to yield repeatedly through the growing season in a manageable amount of space. Sorrel is the perfect example: birds and slugs seem to dislike its acidic leaves, and no matter how harsh the winter it always faithfully reappears, year upon year.

In a really small space, grow bags and and tubs offer a great alternative to the open ground. Herbs and 'cut and come again' lettuce leaves thrive in window boxes, with the added benefit of a picturesque display.

Rhubarb

A grow your own must-have. Rhubarb thrives even in the darkest corner of the garden, it takes care of itself and a mature plant will faithfully produce beautiful pink stems full of goodness year after year from early spring onwards.

Tart and clean-tasting, it works well in both sweet and savoury dishes. Poach with a slit vanilla pod and sugar to taste, to accompany milky puddings, or roast with a drizzle of honey, orange zest and grated ginger root and serve with oily fish, duck or home-cooked ham. Bake in a crumble or simmer with strawberries until soft and combine in a trifle.

Carefully twist the stem from the plant and discard the leaf (sadly, it's only good for the compost heap). To peel, trim both ends, insert the blade of a small knife just under the skin and gently pull the skin away, repeating until all the skin is removed. Rhubarb contains a lot of water, so only a splash of water is necessary when cooking. It's very acidic, so always use a stainless steel or non-reactive saucepan.

At the height of the rhubarb season, freeze excess fruit in prepared chunks or transform into jam or chutney (see recipe for gooseberry chutney, page 111).

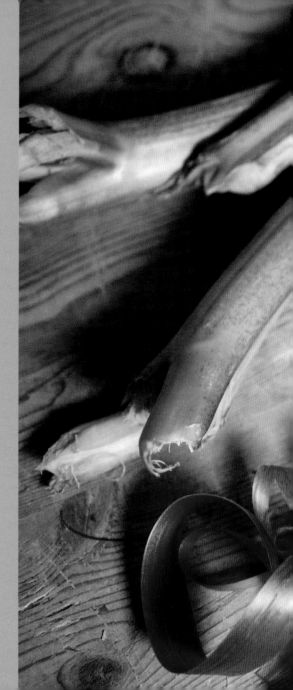

RHUBARB AND CINNAMON PUFFS

Free-form individual puff pastry tarts are so easy to make.
Serve hot from the oven with cream.

MAKES 6 TARTS

5 peeled rhubarb stems
275g/10oz ready-rolled puff pastry
runny honey or agave syrup
ground cinnamon
brown sugar
a little whole milk

Preheat the oven to 200°C/400°F/gas mark 6.

Cut the prepared rhubarb into 5mm/¼ inch slices.

Cut the ready-rolled pastry into 6 portions and place on a baking tray, leaving enough room for the pastry to spread.

Divide the rhubarb equally between the pastry portions. Fold the edges of the pastry up over the rhubarb, leaving the centre uncovered. Pinch the pastry together at regular intervals to keep it in place.

Drizzle the rhubarb with honey or agave syrup to taste, and sprinkle with a little ground cinnamon and brown sugar.

Brush the pastry with milk and bake in a preheated oven for 20–25 minutes, until golden brown.

RHUBARB, GINGER AND CARDAMOM JAM

A heady, slightly sloppy jam, simple and rewarding to make. Spoon on to ice cream, natural yoghurt or warm buttered scones. Rhubarb is low in pectin: the jam sugar and lemon in this recipe help the setting process.
If you prefer your jam tart you can reduce the amount of added sugar a little, but the jam will need to be cooked for longer.

MAKES ABOUT 4 x 450G/1LB JARS

1kg/2¼lb rhubarb, peeled and chopped into 2.5cm/1inch chunks
900g/4½ cups sugar
juice and zest of a lemon
a thumb-sized piece of ginger root, peeled and grated
8 cardamom pods, seeds removed and crushed

Place the prepared rhubarb in a large heavy-bottomed stainless steel saucepan and combine with the sugar, lemon, grated ginger and cardamom. Leave to stand for a couple of hours (you can leave this stage out if you are in a hurry, but it does draw out the juice from the rhubarb).

Put the pan on the stove and bring the rhubarb mixture to the boil, stirring regularly to prevent it sticking. Boil for 20 minutes or so, until the setting point is reached (see page 9).

Pour the hot jam into sterilized jars, top with a waxed jam disc and seal immediately.

Sorrel

This prolific lemony garden herb has been cultivated for centuries, but is still relatively rare in shops. It adds a pleasing distinctively fresh flavour to a meal. The long broad-leafed variety, similar in appearance to spinach, is my choice for cooking, whereas delicate heart shaped buckler sorrel is perfect for salads. Both varieties are easy to grow and are pretty much pest-free; they reappear in spring without fail and by midsummer would happily take over the herb garden. Sadly they die back as winter starts to bite.

Sorrel is particularly good with eggs and fish: a finely chopped handful transforms an omelette batter or a buttery hollandaise sauce. Add a couple of handfuls to a leek and potato soup just before liquidizing or thinly slice and stir into a fish pie filling or (my favourite) wilt a little chopped sorrel in hot seasoned melted butter and coat baby new potatoes, carrots or broad beans.

SORREL, CHARD AND RICOTTA CHEESE PUFF PASTRY PIE

Who can ever resist puff pastry?

2 large handfuls of sorrel leaves
275g/10oz trimmed chard leaves
1 tablespoon salted butter
2 tablespoons olive oil
1 medium onion, diced
2 garlic cloves, finely chopped
salt and black pepper
375g/13oz ready-rolled puff pastry
250g/9oz ricotta cheese
1 small handful of chopped dill leaves
1 small free-range egg, beaten

Preheat the oven to 200°C/400°F/ gas mark 6.

Thinly slice the sorrel and chard leaves and set to one side.

Heat the butter and olive oil in a large saucepan. When the butter has melted add the onion and garlic and sauté until soft.

Add the sliced chard and sorrel leaves and stir together over a low heat until the leaves have wilted to half their original volume. Season to taste.

Grease a medium pie dish with butter and line with ready-rolled pastry. Roughly cut a lid from the remaining pastry.

Spoon the chard mixture into the prepared pie dish, sprinkle chopped dill over the top and cover with ricotta cheese.

Brush the pie edges with beaten egg and carefully place the puff pastry lid on top. Cut away any excess pastry and firmly crimp the edges together. Brush the pie with beaten egg and bake in a preheated oven for 20–25 minutes, until it is golden.

SORREL HOLLANDAISE SAUCE

Dollop thick buttery hollandaise sauce seasoned with lemony sorrel on to fish,
poached eggs or plump spears of asparagus.
Hollandaise has a reputation for being temperamental, but stick to this fail-
safe recipe and you will make perfect sauce every time.

3 large free-range egg yolks
200g/2 sticks melted salted butter
1 tablespoon cold water
1 dessertspoon lemon juice
a handful of thinly sliced sorrel leaves
salt and black pepper

A third fill a smallish saucepan with water and bring the water to a gentle simmer. Select a heatproof bowl that sits comfortably in the pan without touching the simmering water. It is important that the sauce doesn't get too hot or the eggs will curdle, so ensure the water never boils.

Place the egg yolks in the heat-proof bowl with 1 tablespoon of cold water and whisk until frothy. Place the bowl over the simmering water and whisk continuously until the eggs thicken. Whisk in the melted butter a little at a time until all the butter has been incorporated and the sauce is thick and creamy. It is really important never to stop whisking when adding the butter. If, despite all your precautions, the sauce curdles, whisk in a tablespoon of cold water.

Remove the bowl from the pan and whisk in the lemon juice and sliced sorrel. Season to taste and serve as soon as possible.

Rocket

A little packet of seeds goes a long way, producing a prolific 'cut and come again' crop that continues to grow right up to the cold winter months.

Rocket certainly packs a punch for such a small leaf, bursting with hot peppery flavour. The whole plant is edible, flowers and all, so nothing is wasted. I always grow wild rocket as it seems less susceptible to bugs and it comes back bigger and better the following year.

Though rocket tends to wilt quite quickly once picked, soaking in cold water soon perks up the leaves. Store the drained rocket leaves in the fridge in a self-sealing plastic bag.

We all know a handful of rocket leaves livens any salad but how about adding finely chopped rocket to soft cream cheese, mayonnaise or creamy mashed potato? Wilt into hot pasta coated with garlic and chilli butter, fill a cheese omelette with a generous handful just before folding, or use it to top toasted crusty bread rubbed with a peeled garlic clove, drizzled with olive oil and layered with ripe tomato slices. Rocket loses its pungency when cooked. If you want a a stronger flavour, you should barely cook the leaves; or if you have to cook them for longer, use larger quantities.

ROCKET, MUSHROOM AND FETA FILO PASTRY ROLLS

A movable feast, perfect for picnics.

MAKES 6

150g/5oz rocket leaves
2 tablespoons olive oil
1 medium onion, diced
1 garlic clove, crushed
175g/6oz finely diced
  chestnut mushrooms
175g/1½ cups crumbled feta cheese

a handful of pine nuts
salt and black pepper
ready-made filo pastry
  sheets
a little melted butter
beaten egg
sesame seeds

Preheat the oven to 190°C/375°F/gas mark 5.

Finely chop the rocket leaves and set to one side.

Heat the olive oil in a frying pan. Add the onion and garlic and sauté until soft. Add the diced mushrooms and continue to cook until soft. Allow the mixture to cool a little, then combine with the crumbled feta cheese, pine nuts, rocket and seasoning to taste.

Unroll the filo pastry on a large wooden board and carefully brush the top sheet with the melted butter. Spoon a sixth of the mushroom mixture in a fat sausage shape in the middle of the nearest short end of the filo, fold in the sides and tightly roll.

Brush the filo roll with beaten egg, using a little to seal the roll, and sprinkle with sesame seeds.

Place the completed rolls on a greased non-stick baking tray and bake in the preheated oven for 20 minutes.

ROCKET VICHYSSOISE

A cooling peppery soup for a hot summer's day.

110g/4oz rocket leaves
3 medium leeks
2 medium potatoes
1 plump garlic clove
3 tablespoons olive oil
1 litre/4 cups stock
salt and black pepper
75ml/¼ cup double cream
a little extra chopped rocket and cream
   to garnish the soup

Thinly slice the rocket (there is no need to cut away the stalks as the soup will be liquidized).

Slit the leeks lengthwise and wash away any mud or grit; trim each end and thinly slice. Peel and dice the potatoes and crush the garlic clove.

Heat the olive oil in a heavy-bottomed saucepan. Add the leeks, potatoes and crushed garlic, stir until coated with oil, cover the pan and gently sweat the vegetables over a low heat until soft but not brown.

Pour in the stock and simmer together until the potatoes are soft. Turn off the heat and allow the soup to cool until hand temperature. Add the chopped rocket and blend the soup in batches in a liquidizer until smooth. Season to taste.

Pour the soup into a tub and when cold chill in the fridge. Combine with the cream just before serving. Garnish with a swirl of extra cream and chopped rocket.

Chillies

If you have any space on a sunny windowsill, make room for a handsome chilli plant. Nothing beats picking a home-grown chilli.

At chilli festivals I am often overwhelmed by the variety of plants available, the versatility of the beautiful fruit and the passion it inspires. Chillies don't have to be burning hot, they can also be mellow and full of flavour. Choose a variety that suites your taste.

A chilli perks up a simple curry but, stuffed with grated mature cheddar cheese mixed with chopped coriander and grilled until blackened, chillis are sublime. A little chopped chilli transforms mussels, prawns or even oysters. For a chocolate bar with a fiery kick, stir chopped chilli into melted dark chocolate, spread on a tray and allow to cool; or add to ice cream for a hot but cool creamy sensation.

Thread excess harvested chillies on cotton and hang until dry; or add to a bottle of olive oil along with a few coriander seeds, peppercorns and a couple of bay leaves. Whole chillies also freeze remarkably well.

CHILLI AND LIME
ICE CREAM

Strangely — lip-smackingly good!

grated zest and juice of
  2 limes
2 largish red chillies,
  finely chopped
200g/1 cup caster sugar
600ml/2½ cups double cream,
  lightly whipped (still slightly
  sloppy)

Place the lime zest and juice, chopped chilli and castor sugar with a splash of water in a small pan and stir together over a low heat until the sugar has dissolved.

When the chilli syrup has cooled, combine with the cream and spoon into a freezer-proof plastic container. Place in the freezer.

After 2 hours, remove the tub and break up any icy bits with a fork (this prevents the ice cream freezing into a solid block). Repeat the process 2 or 3 times, until the cream has frozen through.

CHILLI AND CIDER MUSSELS

A steaming bowl of spiced mussels, ready in minutes.
Mop up the sauce with thick slices of buttered crusty bread.
To avoid overcooking the mussels, have all the ingredients ready at hand,
to add in quick succession.

2.5kg/5½lb mussels
2 tablespoons olive oil
1 generous tablespoon butter
1 medium shallot, diced
3 garlic cloves, crushed
3 finely sliced red chillies
200ml/¾ cup dry cider, preferably still scrumpy
110ml/½ cup hot vegetable stock
a large handful of finely chopped flat-leaf parsley
salt

Tip the mussels into a large bowl of water, remove any beards and scrape any barnacles from the shells. Wash the mussels a couple of times.

Heat the olive oil and butter in a large saucepan. When the butter melts, add the diced shallot, garlic and chilli and sauté until soft but not brown.

Add the mussels, cider, stock, parsley and seasoning to taste. Cover the pan, turn up the heat and rapid cook the mussels, shaking the pan, for 3–4 minutes. When the mussels are open they are ready to eat. Serve immediately, discarding any mussels that have not opened.

Jerusalem Artichokes

I am breaking my own rule a little here, as mature Jerusalem artichoke plants are very tall and spread like wildfire. However, on a positive note, they require hardly any tending (apart from tying up a rogue shoot or two) and thrive in poor soil even in low light conditions. A member of the sunflower family, they also provide a display of bright sunshine yellow flowers at the end of the summer, when everything is looking a little tired.

You can start harvesting the tubers in the autumn: just dig the light brown knobbly tubers up. But the best way to store Jerusalem artichokes is in the ground (just like buried treasure). They are fine left in the soil through the winter months; in fact it is considered best to harvest the tubers after the first frost. Cut back the stems as they die back and simply dig up when needed. By springtime any tubers left in the ground will start to sprout and multiply to provide next year's crop.

The nutty sweet tubers can be cut into matchsticks and eaten raw in salads, roasted with butter and thyme, pan-fried with chopped garlic and olive oil, mashed or added to soups. Once they are peeled, immerse the tubers in cold water with an added squeeze of lemon juice to avoid the tubers discolouring.

JERUSALEM ARTICHOKE AND
TRUFFLE OIL PURÉE

Earthy truffle oil works just brilliantly with Jerusalem artichokes. Truffle oil varies in strength depending on brand, so I suggest adding the oil to taste. Smear the purée artistically on a plate and top with scallops or white fish pan-fried in butter.

600g/1lb 5oz Jerusalem artichokes
a squeeze of lemon juice
a good knob of butter
2 crushed garlic cloves
a few sprigs of thyme
vegetable stock
110ml/½ cup crème fraîche
salt and black pepper
truffle oil

Peel and dice the Jerusalem artichokes and drop into a bowl of water with a squeeze of lemon juice until ready to use.

Melt a knob of butter in a saucepan, add the garlic and sauté until soft.

Add the drained artichokes, the thyme sprigs and enough vegetable stock to barely cover the vegetables. Cover the pan and simmer until the stock has reduced and the artichokes are soft, adding a little extra water if necessary.

Place the cooked artichokes, thyme and crème fraîche in a food processor and blend until smooth. Season the purée and stir in the truffle oil, starting with half a capful and adding extra to taste.

Drizzle over a little extra oil to serve.

WARM JERUSALEM ARTICHOKE
AND OYSTER MUSHROOM SALAD

Walnut oil and oyster mushrooms complement the nutty flavour of
Jerusalem artichokes. Pile this warm salad on to bitter leaves and
top with crispy fried Parma ham.

600g/1lb 5oz Jerusalem artichokes
6 slices Parma ham
olive oil
a good knob of butter
2 shallots, diced
2 crushed garlic cloves
175g/6oz oyster mushrooms, sliced
2 tablespoons olive oil
1 tablespoon walnut oil
1 tablespoon lemon juice
1 teaspoon grainy mustard
1 dessertspoon finely chopped rosemary leaves
salt and black pepper
bitter leaves, such as radicchio or endive mixed with green salad leaves

Peel the artichokes and simmer in salted boiling water until soft. Drain and return
the artichokes to the warm pan until ready to combine with the dressing.

Fry the Parma ham slices in a little olive oil until crispy and set to one side. Add
the butter to the same frying pan. Add the shallots and garlic and sauté until soft.
Add the sliced oyster mushrooms and lightly fry until just cooked.

Whisk the olive oil, walnut oil, lemon juice, mustard and rosemary together
and season to taste.

Cut the cooked artichokes into thickish slices and combine with the mushrooms
and dressing. Pile the salad on to the bitter leaves and top with the crispy fried
Parma ham.

Chard

Not only is chard officially one of the most nutritious vegetables around, it is also easy to grow and very productive. The more you pick, the more it grows. Deep green and leafy, with striking white, yellow, fuchsia pink or ruby red stems, it makes a beautiful addition to any garden. Chard has an enviably long season and even tolerates a cold winter. As a biennial plant, if it does die back, new leaves will miraculously reappear in early spring to produce a second crop.

Tiny raw young leaves are perfect to toss with a green salad and when mature the leaves still only require a short cooking time. The stems do take a little longer to cook: cut away and cook for a few minutes first before adding the leaves. Plunge into boiling water until the leaves wilt, or – even better – steam, dress with a glug of olive oil whisked with a little balsamic vinegar or (take the uncomplicated route) a large knob of butter and a sprinkling of sea salt or a coating of cream. Chard can be used in a similar way to spinach, with the added bonus of a slightly more robust leaf that doesn't shrink quite so much when cooked, making it a versatile ingredient in pies (see page 53), stir-fries and hearty stews. To maintain chard's optimum nutrition, take care not to overcook the leaves.

The following recipes also work well with kale.

CHARD WITH SAGE, CREAM AND NUTMEG

Creamy chard, seasoned with sage and nutmeg, makes a delicious side dish to any fish or meat; or try combined with pasta (especially tagliatelle).

700g/1½lb chard
2 large knobs of butter
3 garlic cloves, finely chopped
a modest handful of sage leaves,
  finely chopped
300ml/1¼ cups crème fraîche
nutmeg
salt and black pepper

Cut the chard stems and leaves into thickish strips, taking care to keep the stems separate.

Steam or blanch the chard until wilted, cooking the stems for a couple of minutes before adding the leaves.

Melt a good knob of butter in a largish pan and sauté the garlic until golden brown. Add the shredded sage and cook for a minute or so. Add the steamed chard and stir until coated in the flavoured butter.

Spoon in the crème fraîche, add a good grate of nutmeg and season to taste. Gently simmer until the cream has reduced a little to make a sauce.

SPICED CHARD WITH CHICKPEAS

Serve with new potatoes or rice or just pile on buttered toast and top with a poached or fried egg. A side of thick-sliced spicy chorizo sausage sautéed until crunchy also enhances the smoky flavours of this dish.

400g/14oz chard
400g/14oz tin chickpeas
4 tablespoons olive oil
1 medium red onion, diced
2 garlic cloves, finely chopped
1 red pepper, diced
2 medium courgettes, cubed
a pinch of chilli flakes
1 teaspoon ground coriander
1 scant teaspoon pimentón (smoked paprika)
2 plum tomatoes, diced
a handful of chopped coriander leaves
salt and black pepper

Thinly slice the chard stems and leaves, taking care to keep the sliced stems separate.

Drain and rinse the chickpeas.

Heat the olive oil in a wok, add the onion, garlic and red pepper and stir-fry until they start to soften. Add the cubed courgettes and the sliced chard stems and continue to stir-fry until soft.

Add the spices and stir-fry for a minute or so.

Add the diced tomatoes, the chickpeas and the sliced chard leaves. Continue to cook until the chard has wilted and any juice from the tomatoes has reduced. Stir in the chopped coriander and season to taste.

Gluts

'You can never have too much of a good thing' is my mantra. There are times in the year when seasonal produce can become overwhelming. But – what a luxury! There are lots of ways to make the most of seasonal gluts, when a crop is plentiful and good value in the market or your veg patch is booming.

And if all else fails never underestimate the value of a large freezer!

Broad Beans

I always look forward to early summer, when broad beans are piled high and cheap. Full of nutrition, they are one of the oldest cultivated crops in the world.

In Italy, France and Spain, immature finger-size broad beans are eaten whole, pods and all. If you are growing your own, have a try: top and tail the pods, slice in between the small beans, and simmer with crushed garlic and a little stock until soft. Dress the cooked pods with olive oil, lemon juice and finely chopped parsley.

When broad beans are young and tender, you can simply add a knob of butter. Or try some simple flavour combinations, such as combining blanched baby beans with olive oil, rocket leaves and crumbled feta. Or you can add blanched beans to risottos; or make a quick pasta sauce by sautéing onion, chilli and garlic in olive oil, and adding a good measure of double cream, a handful of parsley and some lightly cooked broad beans.

Later in the season, when the beans are larger and the skins thicker, they are best added to stews (see page 126) or puréed to make dips.

Podded broad beans freeze well. Just blanch the beans for 1 minute, before storing in bags in the freezer.

BROAD BEAN AND CUMIN PURÉE WITH CHICORY

A good recipe for larger, end-of-season beans. Serve warm as an appetiser, in the Italian way, topped with sautéed chicory and crusty bread dipped in olive oil, or allow to cool and eat hummus style with toasted pitta.

450g/1lb podded broad beans
 (about 1.35kg/3lb whole beans)
1 teaspoon cumin seeds
3 bay leaves
2 garlic cloves, sliced
6 tablespoons olive oil
3 tablespoons lemon juice
1 flat teaspoon ground cumin
1 flat teaspoon sweet paprika

a handful of mint leaves, chopped
salt and black pepper

2 heads of chicory, sliced
olive oil
2 garlic cloves, crushed
a large handful of chard leaves, sliced

To serve
extra olive oil and cumin seeds

Place the beans in a saucepan along with the cumin seeds, bay leaves and sliced garlic. Add enough water to just cover the beans. Simmer until soft, then drain through a fine sieve, reserving the cooking liquid.

Discard the bay leaves and transfer the sieved ingredients to a food processor. Add the olive oil, lemon juice, cumin, paprika and 3 tablespoons of reserved liquid and blend until a rough purée forms. Stir in the chopped mint and season to taste.

Heat a splash of olive oil in a wok or large frying pan, add the crushed garlic and stir-fry until soft. Throw in the sliced chicory and chard leaves and quickly stir-fry until wilted.

Scoop the warm purée on to a flat serving dish or plate, level and drizzle with extra olive oil. Pile the chicory mixture on top and sprinkle with cumin seeds to taste.

BROAD BEANS BAKED WITH ASPARAGUS

Tender new-season beans are essential for this recipe. Serve with buttered new potatoes sprinkled with chopped fresh mint.

500g/1lb 2oz podded broad beans
(approx 1.5kg/3lb 5oz whole
broad beans)
225g/8oz fine asparagus
1 tablespoon olive oil
2 crushed garlic cloves
125g/4½oz sliced pancetta
6 sliced spring onions
6 large free-range eggs

75ml/¼ cup thick double cream
75ml/¼ cup whole milk
75g/1 cup finely grated pecorino or
Parmesan cheese
a handful of chopped marjoram
leaves
a handful of chopped chives
salt and black pepper
butter

Preheat the oven to 190°C/375°F/gas mark 5.

Cook the broad beans in seasoned boiling water for a few minutes, drain, refresh with cold water and set to one side.

Wash the asparagus and remove the tough ends by bending each stalk until it reaches the position where it naturally wants to snap.

Heat the olive oil in a frying pan. Add the garlic and pancetta and sauté until the garlic is golden and the pancetta is beginning to crisp. Add the spring onions and turn in the oil until they start to wilt. Remove the pan from the heat.

Whisk the eggs, cream and milk together in a bowl. Stir in the grated cheese, chopped marjoram and chives and seasoning to taste. Add the fried pancetta mixture and the blanched broad beans.

Butter a round shallow baking dish, deep enough for the mixture to fit snugly inside (approx 30cm/12 inches). Pour in the mixture, making sure the beans and pancetta are evenly distributed, and carefully lay the asparagus nose to tail on top.

Bake in the preheated oven for 30 minutes, until just set and golden brown – it should still have a bit of a wobble when gently shaken.

Allow to cool for 5 minutes before cutting (if you try any earlier you run the risk of collapse).

Tomatoes

Thankfully, the days of uniform pale red tomatoes with barely any flavour dominating the market are coming to an end. Ruby red, yellow, orange, green, cherry, plum, beef and grape tomatoes are now making their presence felt: beautiful heritage varieties each with its own unique flavour, texture and shape.

Choose sweet cherry or grape tomatoes for salads or roasting; plum tomatoes are perfect for rich tomato sauces and thickly sliced beef tomatoes just seem to have been made to accompany soft, creamy mozzarella cheese.

A tomato should smell like a tomato: the more intense the scent the more intense the flavour. Proudly choose tomatoes that are irregular in shape – if they are a little green in part, they will soon ripen once home. Tomatoes are best stored out of the fridge and served when fully ripe and succulent.

Tomatoes are so versatile, it is quite easy to eat them every day without getting bored. There are so many simple combinations that hardly warrant a recipe. Serve chunks of multicoloured varieties coated with olive oil and sprinkled with crushed sea salt and black pepper; maybe add a drizzle of balsamic vinegar and Parmesan one day or fresh herbs another – I would choose from basil, oregano, marjoram or thyme. Layer thick slices of tomatoes, avocado and mozzarella and top with torn basil and seasoned olive oil. Mix cubed tomatoes with cucumber, fresh mint and parsley leaves and crumble salty feta cheese over the top. Dowse whole cherry tomatoes with olive oil and chopped garlic and bake in a hot oven until their juices release or pop inside a halved pepper, spoon wild garlic pesto over the top and bake in a hot oven until soft. Whizz tomatoes in a blender with crushed garlic, sliced spring onions, a good measure of olive oil, a splash of port, a dash of Worcester sauce and lots of fresh basil and chill in the fridge for a cooling soup on a hot summer's day. Or sweat tomatoes with diced onion and garlic, simmer with seasoned stock and blend with marjoram leaves for a warming soup when the weather is less clement. Sweet and intense semi-dried sun-blushed tomatoes can be stored for months simply covered with olive oil. Halve tomatoes, season and slow roast, on the lowest heat setting of the oven, for 3 hours until semi-dried. Transfer to a jar, pour over some olive oil and seal. They can be tossed later with salads or pasta, or baked in tarts and bread.

STRAWBERRY, RHUBARB AND SPINACH SALAD

Sweet strawberries, crisp raw rhubarb, baby spinach and watercress leaves tossed with balsamic dressing and topped with pine nuts and Parmesan shavings.

1 punnet of strawberries (roughly 450g/1lb)
2 prepared rhubarb stems
a couple of handfuls of young leaf spinach
a couple of handfuls of watercress
a handful of toasted pine nuts
Parmesan shavings

Dressing
3 tablespoons olive oil
2 tablespoons balsamic vinegar
1 teaspoon clear honey
a squeeze of fresh lemon juice
salt and black pepper

Hull the strawberries and cut into quarters. Thinly slice the prepared rhubarb.

Mix the spinach and watercress together in a bowl and scatter with the rhubarb and strawberries.

Whisk the dressing ingredients together, season to taste and drizzle evenly over the salad.

Sprinkle with the toasted pine nuts and Parmesan shavings.

ETON MESS

There are many stories about how this legendary British pudding was created. My favourite is the tale of how a friendly Labrador dog accidentally sat on a strawberry pavlova at Eton's annual school picnic and made a bit of a 'mess'.
One thing for sure is that we have Eton College to thank for the inspired combination of crushed meringues, soft whipped cream and ripe strawberries. A splash of port added to the crushed strawberries makes a boozy alternative. By all means make your own meringues, but there are many good shop-bought alternatives available.

500g/1lb 2oz ripe strawberries, hulled
a splash of port (optional)
600ml/2½ cups double cream
a few drops of vanilla extract
about 6 large meringues

Reserve 6 strawberries to decorate the pudding.
Place half the strawberries in a bowl (with a splash of port, if you like) and crush with a fork until roughly mashed. Quarter the remaining strawberries.
Whisk the cream with a few drops of vanilla extract until floppy peaks form.
Place the meringues in a plastic bag and lightly crush with a rolling pin until broken into chunks (you don't want the meringue pieces to be too small or they will completely dissolve in the cream).
Just before serving, roughly fold the crushed and quartered strawberries, cream and meringue chunks together until a marbled effect forms.
Spoon into glasses and decorate with strawberry quarters. Serve immediately.

Runner Beans

In midsummer there are always bundles of runner beans by the allotment gate, free for passers-by to take home. The runner bean plant literally runs away with itself and at up to 2 metres/6 feet tall it is destined to be the king of gluts. The more the merrier: at their best runner beans are tender, full of flavour and brimming with protein.

Biggest isn't always best: runner beans become stringy when allowed to grow too long. Choose medium-sized beans that are firm and snap easily. String the beans by peeling each side with a vegetable peeler and thinly slice on a diagonal. Any prepared beans can also be blanched and frozen.

Nothing beats a pile of beans covered in gravy, but how about making a warm salad? Mix sliced blanched beans with halved cherry tomatoes, chopped basil, toasted pine nuts and a simple vinaigrette. For an easy side dish, simmer thinly cut beans in garlic butter with a dash of double cream or toss with pesto and grated Parmesan cheese. However you choose to enjoy them, remember they only need a short cooking time.

French beans can replace runner beans in all of these recipes.

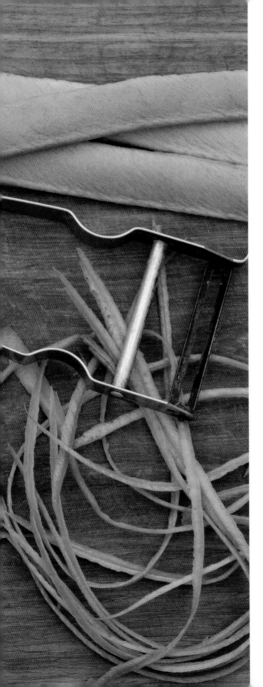

SPICED RUNNER BEANS

Runner beans cooked with aromatic spices make an unusual side dish to serve with grilled meat or rice dishes.

500g/1lb 2oz runner beans or French beans
1 teaspoon ground cumin
1 teaspoon ground coriander
1 teaspoon garam masala
½ teaspoon ground turmeric
1 teaspoon clear honey
3 tablespoons sunflower oil
½ teaspoon cumin seeds
1 teaspoon black mustard seeds
a pinch of chilli flakes
3 medium tomatoes, diced
salt and black pepper

Top and tail the beans, string and slice thinly diagonally. Blanch the prepared beans in a pan of boiling water for a couple of minutes, drain and refresh with cold water.

Mix the 4 ground spices together and combine with the clear honey and enough water to make a thinnish paste.

Heat the oil in a thick-bottomed saucepan. Add the cumin seeds, mustard seeds and chilli flakes. When the seeds pop add the honey spice mix and stir-fry for 30 seconds. Add the chopped tomatoes and simmer for 5 minutes.

Add the blanched beans, season to taste and simmer on a low heat for a further 5 minutes.

RUNNER BEANS WITH NEW POTATOES, PESTO AND SPAGHETTI

Potatoes and pasta might seem an odd combination, but trust me it works. Traditionally the same water is used to cook all the ingredients. Wild garlic pesto (page 13) works well in this recipe; alternatively, you can use a good-quality shop-bought basil pesto. Feel free to play around with the recipe, I sometimes add broad beans or peas and reduce the amount of runner beans.

350g/12oz runner or French beans
5 smallish waxy new potatoes (about 275g/10oz),
   such as Jersey Royals or salad potatoes
300g/11oz spaghetti
5 heaped tablespoons pesto
a handful of sliced black olives
salt and black pepper
olive oil
grated Parmesan cheese

Top and tail the beans, string and thinly slice diagonally. Peel and dice the new potatoes.

Bring a large pan of salted water to the boil. Add the sliced beans and cook for a few minutes until just soft. Remove the beans with a slotted spoon and set to one side.

Bring the water back to the boil, add the potatoes and simmer until soft, but not breaking down. Remove the potatoes with a slotted spoon and add to the cooked beans.

Bring the water back to the boil again, add the spaghetti and boil until al dente (cooked but not soft). Drain the pasta, reserving 110ml/½ cup of the cooking liquid.

Return the reserved drained water to the pan, and add the pesto, sliced olives and seasoning to taste. When the sauce starts to simmer add the cooked spaghetti, potato and beans. Gently stir together until well combined and piping hot.

Serve drizzled with extra olive oil and a generous serving of grated Parmesan cheese.

Courgettes

At the height of summer plump courgettes are abundant. Thanks to farmers' markets, along with conventional dark green varieties, eye-catching yellow, pale green and stripped courgettes are also available. If you are thinking of growing your own, even one modest plant produces a decent quantity of fruit.

Choose small to medium-sized courgettes. Their tender skin and flesh is just as good eaten raw as it is lightly cooked. Simple is often best: slice the courgettes thinly lengthwise, brush with seasoned olive oil, chargrill and garnish with chopped mint leaves; or slice thickly and quick-fry with crushed new season's garlic; or just grate and sauté with butter. Ribbons of raw courgette, peeled with the aid of a vegetable peeler, make an attractive addition to any salad.

Courgette flowers are a brief seasonal treat. Tear the flowers into small pieces and add to any courgette recipe. Stuff whole courgette flowers with a spoonful of ricotta or soft goat's cheese combined with chopped basil leaves (see the filling for courgette rolls on page 95), pinch the flower together and flash-fry in olive oil until golden.

COURGETTE, RICOTTA AND BASIL ROLLS

Freshly picked courgettes served raw, thinly sliced and rolled with Parma ham and herby ricotta cheese make tasty and unusual finger food. If any of the courgettes still have their flowers attached, even better. Carefully wash the flower, tear it into pieces and add to the ricotta mixture. Choose yellow courgettes for this recipe if you can: they look very pretty and have a subtler flavour.
The ricotta mixture can also be used to stuff courgette flowers.

3 medium courgettes
225g/8 oz ricotta
1 large red chilli, finely chopped
grated zest of half a lemon
1 tablespoon olive oil
a small handful of basil leaves, finely chopped
courgette flowers, washed and torn into small pieces
salt and black pepper
110g/4oz thinly cut Parma or Serrano ham

Trim the courgettes and thinly slice lengthwise using a vegetable peeler. Discard any outer slices that are mainly skin. Lay the courgettes on a large flat dish and season with a little salt and black pepper.

Combine the ricotta with the chopped chilli, lemon zest, olive oil, chopped basil and courgette flowers. Season to taste.

Cut the ham into slightly thinner strips than the courgette slices.

Lay a strip of ham on top of each courgette slice and spoon a little of the ricotta mixture on to one end. Tightly roll the courgette around the filling. Repeat the process until all the ingredients have been used up. Chill until ready to serve.

COURGETTE AND BANANA CAKE

When you simply cannot face another meal with courgettes, how about a courgette cake? Far more interesting than carrot cake and a handy way to use up larger courgettes. I like to use wholemeal spelt flour, but you can substitute regular wholemeal flour if you prefer.

225g/8oz courgettes
2 bananas
110ml/½ cup sunflower oil
3 medium free-range eggs
100g/½ cup Demerara (raw) sugar
225g/1½ cups wholemeal spelt flour

2 teaspoons baking powder
½ teaspoon salt
½ teaspoon ground cardamom
25g/⅓ cup desiccated coconut
75g/½ cup raisins
sunflower seeds, to sprinkle on top

Preheat the oven to 190°C/375°F/gas mark 5.

Medium-grate the courgettes and squeeze any excess water away with your (clean) hands.

Peel the bananas and mash with a fork until broken down.

Beat the oil, eggs and sugar together until creamy. Fold in the flour, baking powder, salt and cardamom.

Carefully stir in the grated courgette, mashed banana, coconut and raisins.

Turn out into a lined loaf tin and cover the surface of the cake mixture with sunflower seeds.

Bake in the middle of the preheated oven for about an hour. The cake should spring back when lightly pressed in the middle. If it doesn't, cook for a little longer and test again.

Root Vegetables

There is a point in the year when winter seems endless, spring, with its tantalizing colourful crops, seems a very long way away, and root vegetables seem to fill the shelves. But never fear, there is more to these faithful winter staples than meets the eye.

Combine potato and parsnip to create pillowy soft homemade gnocchi. Layer thinly sliced mixed root vegetables of your choice with finely chopped garlic and thyme and bake with cream to create a contemporary twist on a classic dauphinoise (follow the recipe on page 16 as a guide). Add matchsticks of raw baby turnip to coleslaw, or thinly slice the turnip and dress with olive oil, a good squeeze of lemon juice and finely chopped parsley to make a crisp winter side salad. Mash equal quantities of cooked swede and parsnip with mustard, cream and butter and serve with plump herby sausages and caramelized onions. A Sunday roast is incomplete without roast potatoes, but mixed roots tossed with honey and rosemary make a wonderful addition.

PARSNIP GNOCCHI

Once you've tasted homemade gnocchi, there's no going back to ready-made. And the little dumplings are so quick to make, there's no excuse not to have a try. Top with your favourite pasta sauce.

The amount of flour required varies a little, depending on the type of potatoes used. Start with the suggested amount and add extra if necessary.

450g/1lb parsnips
450g/1lb mashing potatoes
200g/1⅓ cups buckwheat or plain flour, plus extra to roll
2 medium free-range egg yolks, beaten
a handful of sage leaves, finely chopped
salt and black pepper

Peel the parsnips and potatoes, cut into largish chunks and cook in simmering salted water until just soft. Drain the vegetables, return to the pan and steam dry over a low heat for a few minutes. Remove from the heat and mash together until smooth. Set to one side and allow to cool.

Combine the mash with the flour, egg yolk, sage and seasoning to taste. Coat the mixture with flour and knead for a few minutes until a dough forms.

Pull away a handful of dough, roll into a thinnish sausage shape on a floured board and cut into 2.5 cm/1 inch bite-size pieces. Repeat until all the dough has been used up.

Drop the prepared gnocchi into a pan of rapidly boiling salted water. The gnocchi are ready when they have all risen to the surface of the water.

ROSEMARY AND HONEY ROASTED ROOTS

Caramelized on the outside, sweet and soft on the inside. Serve with herbed couscous, thick slices of ham or a Sunday roast. You can use any combination of root vegetables – try adding beetroot and Jerusalem artichoke as a seasonal variation.

½ medium swede, peeled and cut into chunks
2 small turnips, peeled and cut into chunks
2 parsnips, peeled and cut into chunks
3 carrots, peeled and quartered lengthwise
½ medium celeriac, peeled and cut into chunks
2 medium red onions, peeled and cut into eighths
1 small head of garlic, broken into cloves and left in their skins
1 generous tablespoon clear honey
olive oil
butter
a small bunch of rosemary, leaves removed from stalks
salt and black pepper

Preheat the oven to 190°C/375°F/gas mark 5.

Line a large roasting pan with the prepared vegetables. Drizzle with a good amount of olive oil (enough to coat the roots without leaving them swimming in a pool of oil). Add the honey and massage the vegetables with your clean hands until they are well coated with the oil and honey.

Dot with a little butter, scatter the rosemary leaves over the top and season to taste.

Bake in a preheated oven, turning the vegetables a couple of times, for 55 minutes or so, until they are caramelized and golden brown.

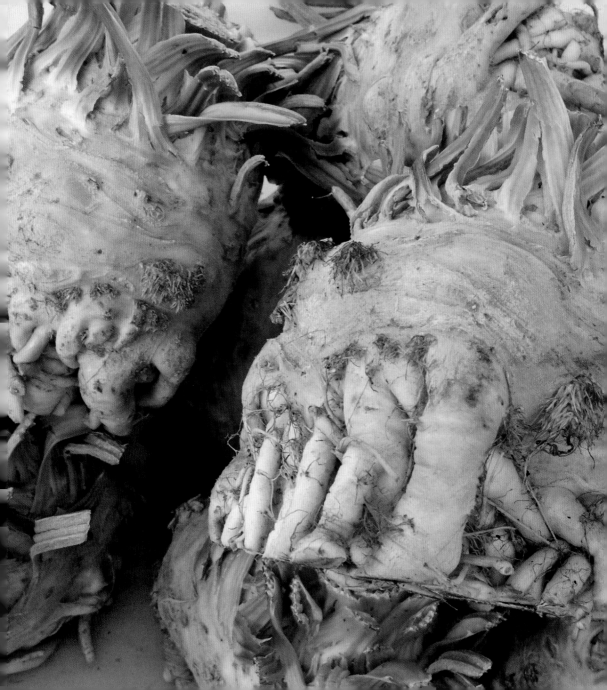

What on Earth do I do with This?

When I started having a regular 'veg box' delivery and shopping at local markets, through the seasons I gradually became aware of rather strange, alien-looking fruit and vegetables that I had never had the pleasure of cooking with before. Long-forgotten gnarled and knobbly favourites, such as quince and celeriac, reintroduced to the marketplace by innovative farmers. Thank goodness for the recipe cards included in the veg box and the helpful advice from enthusiastic market stall holders, who always have a wealth of knowledge and passion for the produce they grow. With a little research and a lot of chatting, I soon became a dab hand at getting the best from these traditional gems.

Celeriac

Celeriac might be the ugly duckling of the vegetable world, but this bulbous knobbly root, derived from the wild celery plant, is secretly a swan on the inside. Its white crunchy flesh, with a hint of celery flavour, becomes silky smooth when cooked. Enjoy raw in salads or roast in a hot oven with olive oil, thyme and chopped garlic. It is particularly good with fruit; simmer in stock with apples or pears, onion and potato to make an innovative soup, or boil and mash with apple chunks caramelized in butter.

One of its many attributes is a very long shelf life. Stored in a cool dark place it keeps for weeks. Returning from holiday it's always a welcome sight in an otherwise empty fridge, a handy ingredient to rustle up a quick homecoming supper.

Cut away the roots, skin and any green shoots and, to avoid discoloration, immerse in cold water with a squeeze of lemon until ready to use.

CELERIAC, FENNEL AND APPLE REMOULADE

Celeriac is as common as the carrot in France and is sold raw in pre-cut matchstick shapes ready to make remoulade, a crunchy salad rather like coleslaw. Apple, fennel and capers are added to the classic recipe to make a remoulade with a contemporary twist. Serve with watercress and prosciutto or smoked fish.

½ medium celeriac (about 275g/10oz)
1 fennel bulb
1 tart apple

Dressing
4 heaped tablespoons good mayonnaise
1 heaped tablespoon Greek yoghurt
1 tablespoon olive oil
juice of half a lemon
2 heaped tablespoons roughly chopped capers
a small handful of chopped flat-leaf parsley
salt and black pepper

Peel the celeriac, cut into matchstick shapes, and immerse in cold water with a splash of lemon juice until ready to use. Trim the fennel, cut in half lengthwise, remove the hard central core and thinly slice. Core the apple, cut it into matchsticks and add to the lemon water along with the celeriac.

Whisk the dressing ingredients together and season to taste.

Drain the celeriac and apple, pat dry with a clean tea towel and combine with the fennel. Toss with the dressing until well coated.

CELERIAC CHAMP

Celeriac adds a nutty flavour to this St Patrick's Day favourite, traditionally made from potato mashed with spring onions and topped with butter.

1 medium celeriac, peeled and cubed
3 medium mashing potatoes, peeled and cubed
2 garlic cloves, peeled and quartered
110ml/½ cup whole milk
a bunch of spring onions, thinly sliced
a good knob of butter
1 heaped teaspoon grainy mustard
75ml/¼ cup thick double cream or full-fat crème fraîche
a large handful of finely chopped curly parsley
salt and black pepper

To serve
extra butter, at room temperature

Simmer the prepared celeriac, potato and garlic in boiling water until soft. Drain the vegetables, return to the pan and steam dry over a low heat for a few minutes.

Heat the milk and sliced spring onions in a small pan until nearly boiling, reduce the heat and gently simmer for a further couple of minutes.

Add the milk mixture along with the butter and mustard to the drained celeriac and potato. Mash everything together until smooth. Stir in the cream and chopped parsley and season to taste.

To serve in the traditional way, pile the champ into a bowl, make an indent in the top with the back of a serving spoon and fill with a large knob of butter room temperature. Serve immediately as the butter melts.

Gooseberries

Firm, full flavoured and juicy, gooseberries vary in sweetness depending on variety: as a general rule of thumb green tend to be sharper than red.

Popular for centuries in jams, pies, puddings and chutneys, gooseberries are now making a comeback. Tart gooseberry sauce makes a traditional accompaniment to mackerel or oily fish and nothing quite beats a deep filled gooseberry pie or crumble topped with thick creamy custard. Simmer gooseberries with equal quantities of apple and enough water to prevent sticking until the fruit starts to soften, sweeten to taste, pile into a pie dish, top with crumble, shortcrust or puff pastry, and bake in the oven until golden brown.

To prepare gooseberries, trim away any stalks and hairy tufts with a pair of kitchen scissors. Once prepared they require only a short cooking time.

The gooseberry fruiting season is short, but you can freeze prepared uncooked berries whole, to enjoy all year round.

GOOSEBERRY SAUCE

Traditionally served with mackerel, this tart sauce also works well with any oily fish or pork. Incidentally, it is just as good spooned on to thick yoghurt or porridge.

300g/10oz prepared gooseberries
zest and juice of half an orange
a 4cm/1½ inch piece of peeled and
    grated ginger root
1 tablespoon clear honey
a large knob of butter

Place all the ingredients in a saucepan and gently simmer, stirring at regular intervals, until the gooseberries are soft and start to break down.

GOOSEBERRY AND ELDERFLOWER FOOL

By happy chance gooseberries are ready to pick at the same time as elderflowers. Here is a classic example of 'what grows together goes together'. Purists tie a handful of elderflowers in a muslin bag and simmer along with the berries (if using flowers you may need to add a little extra sugar). Alternatively, add a slug of homemade elderflower cordial.

450g/1lb prepared gooseberries
50–100g/¼–½ cup golden caster sugar (to taste)
4 tablespoons elderflower cordial
300ml/1¼ cups double cream
zest of a lime

To decorate
blueberries and mint leaves

Simmer the gooseberries and caster sugar with a tablespoon of water until soft, crushing the berries after a few minutes to encourage them to break down and release their juices. Stir in the elderflower cordial and leave to cool.

Whip the cream until it forms soft peaks. Fold in the cooled crushed gooseberries and lime zest.

Spoon the fool into teacups or glasses, cover with cling film and chill in the fridge for an hour or so. Decorate with blueberries and mint leaves before serving.

GOOSEBERRY CHUTNEY

Serve a farmhouse Cheddar cheese ploughman's with a dollop of this
punchy gooseberry chutney, and you'll never look back.
The recipe also works well with rhubarb. Peel the stems, cut into
chunks and follow the same method.

MAKES ABOUT 2 x 450G/1LB JARS

700g/1½lb prepared gooseberries
1 red onion, finely chopped
1 dessertspoon finely chopped ginger root
110ml/½ cup water
225g/1½ cups brown sugar
½ teaspoon salt
a large handful of raisins
1 flat teaspoon ground ginger
1 cinnamon stick or 1 teaspoon ground cinnamon
¼ teaspoon cayenne pepper
½ teaspoon yellow mustard seeds
¼ teaspoon crushed black pepper
240ml/1 cup cider vinegar

Simmer the gooseberries with the diced onion, chopped ginger and
water until soft. Gently crush the gooseberries with the back of a
wooden spoon.

Add the remaining ingredients and simmer briskly until the chutney
has reduced to a jam-like consistency.

Remove the cinnamon stick and spoon the chutney into sterilized jars.
Seal with a tight-fitting lid and store in a cool, dark place. The chutney
can be eaten straight away but if you can wait it does improve with age.

Beetroot

Beetroot has achieved a revolution. No longer soaked in vinegar and served sliced with a limp lettuce leaf, it has seized its rightful place as a traditional home-grown staple, full of potent antioxidants and minerals. Look out for yellow, orange or pink-and-white-striped varieties.

Sweet and earthy, it is as delicious served raw as it is cooked, and combined with carrots and ginger root it makes a nutrient-packed juice.

Its culinary uses are endless: roast whole baby beets doused in olive oil until soft or layer wafer-thin beetroot slices with grated cheese and cream in a pastry case and bake until golden. Pair cooked beetroot with soft goat's cheese, walnuts, pomegranate seeds and salad leaves or simply slice and serve with horseradish sauce and rocket leaves in a homemade burger.

Choose smallish roots, preferably with the leaves still attached. Don't discard the leaves (beetroot was originally grown for its leaves), mix small tender leaves with salads or steam larger leaves and drizzle with oil.

A medium-sized beetroot takes about 30 minutes to cook in simmering water; trim the stalks away leaving the tapered root and skin intact – the skin easily peels away when cooked. Remember to wear rubber gloves when handling beetroot, if you want to avoid pink-stained hands.

BEETROOT LEAVES WITH WALNUTS, RAISINS AND ORANGE

Beetroot leaves are best used when they are very fresh. Like spinach, they shrink considerably once cooked. Chard or kale can also be used in the place of beetroot leaves.

SERVES 2

fresh leaves cut from a large bunch of beetroot
1 tablespoon olive oil
1 garlic clove, thinly sliced
1 hot red chilli, thinly sliced
2.5cm/1inch peeled ginger root
a handful of chopped walnuts
a handful of raisins
grated zest and juice of half an orange
salt and black pepper
soft goat's cheese, to serve

Thoroughly wash the beetroot leaves (they can often be a bit muddy) and roughly slice.

Heat the oil in a large frying pan, add the garlic, chilli and ginger and stir-fry until soft.

Add the chopped walnuts and raisins and stir-fry until caramelized.

Add the prepared beetroot leaves, orange juice and zest and stir-fry until the leaves are soft.

Season to taste and serve dotted with soft goat's cheese.

BEETROOT BARLEY RISOTTO WITH HORSERADISH CREAM

Beetroot and nutty pearl barley are cooked together to make
a healthy alternative to a traditional risotto.

3 medium raw beetroot
2 tablespoons olive oil
25g/¼ stick butter
1 medium red onion, diced
3 garlic cloves, finely chopped
400g/2 cups pearl barley
110ml/½ cup dry white wine
2 bay leaves
1 litre/4 cups hot chicken
  or vegetable stock
75g/1 cup grated mature Manchego
  or Parmesan cheese

a large knob of butter
a handful of marjoram leaves, chopped
salt and black pepper

To serve
110ml/½ cup crème fraîche or sour
  cream
1 heaped dessertspoon hot horseradish
rocket leaves
extra grated Manchego or Parmesan
  cheese

Wearing rubber gloves, peel and medium-grate the beetroot.

In a heavy-bottomed pan heat the olive oil and butter. When the butter has melted, add the onion and garlic and sauté until soft but not brown.

Add the grated beetroot and the pearl barley and stir until coated in oil.

Pour in the wine and simmer, stirring constantly until absorbed.

Add the bay leaves and a ladle of hot stock and cook on a medium heat, stirring constantly until the stock has been absorbed. Continue adding the stock ladle by ladle, until the stock has been used up and the pearl barley is soft, adding extra stock if necessary.

Remove the bay leaves and stir in the cheese, butter, marjoram and seasoning to taste.

Season the crème fraîche and whisk in the hot horseradish. Spoon on to the risotto and top with grated cheese and rocket leaves.

Quince

'Quince! Help yourself' read the sign on a bucket of unusual-looking pear-shaped fruit, outside a kindly neighbour's house. So I did and after chatting with those in the know I set to. Soon my kitchen was filled with the floral scent of this wonderful ancient fruit.

A relative of the apple and pear tree, quince has a hard flesh with a slightly furry bloom on the skin. Most varieties are inedible when raw, but once cooked they become soft, dark pink and luscious with a perfumed flavour. Use a sturdy vegetable peeler to peel away the tough outer skin and once peeled drop into water with a squeeze of lemon to avoid discoloration. Prepared quince takes about 30 minutes to cook. Its firm flesh holds its shape well and it can easily be frozen for a later date.

Mix poached quince chunks with apples in a crumble or *tarte tatin* or purée together to make a fruity sauce. Add a pinch of cinnamon, star anise, nutmeg or clove to complement its delicate floral flavour. Poach with honey, cinnamon, grated fresh ginger root and orange zest or add to spiced savoury stews. The high pectin content of quince ensures an easy to set jam, jelly or fruit cheese.

QUINCE CHEESE

Serve slices of this thick preserve with mature tangy cheese for a sweet-savoury taste combination. The recipe is for 1kg/2¼lb of quince – adjust the measurements depending on how much fruit you have available.
If you can't get hold of quince, apples mixed with blackberries make a good substitute; sieve the fruit before measuring the required amount of sugar.
To make quince jam, replace the vanilla with the juice and rind of a lemon and briskly simmer the fruit and sugar together for a shorter length of time, until the mixture has the consistency of a jam and setting point is reached (see page 9).

MAKES ABOUT 1KG/2¼LB

1kg/2¼lb quince
150ml/⅔ cup water

sugar
1 vanilla pod, slit lengthwise

Peel the quince and immerse in a bowl of water with a squeeze of lemon until ready to use.

Medium-grate the quince flesh from the central core and place in a heavy-bottomed saucepan. Pour in the water, cover the pan and simmer until the fruit is soft and breaking down.

Allow the quince purée to cool a little, and then pour into a measuring jug. Calculate how much sugar to add based on the proportion of 450g/2¼ cups of sugar for every 600ml/2½ cups of fruit.

Return the quince to the pan with the correct quantity of sugar and stir together over a low heat until all the sugar has dissolved. Scrape the seeds from the slit vanilla pod and add to the pan. Turn up the heat and simmer briskly, stirring regularly, until a thick, dark pink mixture forms. The cheese should be thick enough to leave a clean line when a spoon is drawn across the bottom of the pan.

Allow the quince to cool a little, spoon into medium-sized flat oblong plastic tubs (with a fitted lid) and level with the back of a spoon. When completely cool, cover the tubs and place in the fridge. Quince cheese is ready once it has fully set, although it does benefit from a little age. Stored in the fridge it will keep for weeks.

SPICED CHICKEN CASSEROLE WITH QUINCE

A rich, aromatic spiced one-pot casserole, with the added subtle flavour of scented quince. To make life easy I always use a cast-iron stovetop-to-oven casserole dish. If you don't have such a thing, just use a frying pan on top of the stove and transfer to a casserole dish before placing in the oven.

2 quince
1 medium sweet potato
1 red pepper
2 tablespoons olive oil
6 chicken thighs
1 large red onion, cut into chunks
2 crushed garlic cloves
1 teaspoon ground cumin

1 teaspoon ground coriander
½ teaspoon black pepper
½ teaspoon ground ginger
½ teaspoon ground cinnamon
a handful of black olives
chicken stock
salt

Preheat the oven to 190°C/375°F/gas mark 5.

Peel and core the quince and cut each one lengthwise into 6 pieces. Peel the sweet potato and cut into largish chunks. Cut the pepper in half, de-seed and cut into thickish strips.

Heat the olive oil in a stovetop-to-oven pan and brown the chicken thighs on all sides. Remove the chicken from the pan and set to one side. Add the onion and garlic to the same pan and sauté until just soft. Sprinkle in the spices and cook for a further minute, stirring constantly to prevent sticking.

Turn off the heat and return the chicken to the pan. Add the quince, vegetables and olives. Season with salt to taste and pour in enough stock to half cover the chicken. Cover the pan with a fitted lid or foil.

Place the casserole in the preheated oven for about 1 hour 10 minutes, removing the cover after 45 minutes and basting the vegetables and chicken with the sauce.

Brussels Sprouts

Love them or loathe them there is certainly more to the humble Brussels sprout than being boiled to death. Childhood memories of mushy dull green blobs leaking water on to a plate have given Brussels a bad reputation (a tasteless mass to skirt around and hide under a napkin). With a little age and wisdom I now view these attractive mini cabbages, full of vitamins and folic acid, as something rather special.

The first rule is never to overcook a Brussels sprout. The second is to eat them only when they are naturally in season; they taste sweeter after the first frost.

Serve Brussels sprouts with pride; sauté in butter and garlic or purée with cream and mustard. Baby sprouts are delicate enough to eat raw: finely shred, mix with pea sprouts and toasted pumpkin seeds and dress with a lemony vinaigrette. Older sprouts make a thick and warming winter soup; sauté with chopped onion, potato and chestnuts, cover with stock and simmer until soft. Season with nutmeg and liquidize with a splash of cream.

CREAMY BRUSSELS PURÉE WITH WALNUTS

I defy anyone not to enjoy this creamy, nutty dish served with crispy fried streaky bacon and caramelized onions.

600g/1lb 5oz Brussels sprouts, trimmed and halved
150ml/⅔ cup double cream
1 teaspoon Dijon mustard
a handful of chopped walnuts
a drizzle of walnut oil
salt and black pepper

To serve
crispy fried streaky bacon
1 large red onion, thinly sliced and sautéed with a large knob of butter and a grate of nutmeg until caramelized

Plunge the trimmed Brussels sprouts into simmering water and cook for about 7 minutes, until just soft.

Drain the sprouts and blend in a food processor with the double cream, mustard and chopped walnuts until roughly puréed but not completely smooth. Season to taste.

Serve topped with the caramelized onions and crispy fried bacon.

BRUSSELS STIR-FRY WITH GINGER, CUMIN AND CHILLI

Lightly spiced, beautiful bright green al dente Brussels sprouts. It's also worth adding a handful of thinly sliced chestnuts if available.

700g/1½lb Brussels sprouts
2 tablespoons salted butter
1 tablespoon olive oil
1 scant teaspoon cumin seeds
a thumb-sized piece of ginger root, peeled and cut into julienne strips
1 large red chilli, cut into thin strips
a handful of thinly sliced chestnuts (optional)
light soy sauce
salt and black pepper

Trim the sprouts and remove any discoloured outer leaves. Plunge into a pan of simmering water for a maximum of 4 minutes, drain and refresh in cold water. Pat dry and cut in half.

Heat the butter and olive oil in a wok. When the butter melts add the cumin seeds. As soon as the seeds start to pop add the ginger and chilli and stir-fry for a couple of minutes.

Add the sprouts (and chestnuts) and continue to stir-fry until the sprouts are caramelized on the outside but still al dente in the middle. Serve dressed with a splash of soy sauce and seasoning to taste.

Kale

Kale has always been a favourite crop for the cottage garden. The ornamental plant soldiers on through the harshest of winters to provide much-needed 'cut and come again' greens, an enviable quality that has guaranteed kale a home in veg box deliveries and farmers' markets.

A member of the cabbage family, kale comes in many varieties, with beautiful curly or serrated leaves in exotic shades of purple, violet and green. Its leaf has a tough central stem that needs to be cut away before cooking and it is best to blanch the robust leaves before adding to recipes.

Toss roughly chopped blanched kale with sliced crispy fried garlic and pancetta or for a more oriental flavour stir-fry with sliced shitake mushrooms, cubed tofu, julienne ginger root, chopped chilli and a good shake of soy sauce. Kale is also an essential ingredient in the traditional Irish dish colcannon; mash cooked potatoes with thinly sliced steamed kale, chopped spring onions, cream and butter. I also add raw kale to a super food smoothie (more delicious than it sounds, I promise!): for two people liquidize a handful of sliced leaves (central stem removed) with a banana, a handful of blueberries and strawberries, a dollop of yoghurt, some grated fresh ginger and a wine glass of still water.

CRISPY SEAWEED

Yes, crispy seaweed is in fact curly kale! The kale leaves can be deep-fried but roasting the thinly sliced leaves in a hot oven is a much healthier option. Serve as a side dish to any stir-fry. Once cooked, crispy seaweed keeps well in an airtight container for several days.

300g/11oz kale leaves
3 garlic cloves, finely chopped
1 tablespoon sesame oil
1 tablespoon rapeseed or sunflower oil
1 dessertspoon sesame seeds
salt

Preheat the oven to 200°C/400°F/gas mark 6.

Strip the kale leaves from the central stem and thinly slice. Tip the leaves into a large bowl, add the chopped garlic, oil and salt to taste and massage the ingredients together with your hands until all the kale is coated in oil.

Spread on to a large flat baking tray and place on the top shelf of a preheated oven. After 5 minutes turn the kale. After another 5 minutes turn again and sprinkle with the sesame seeds. Return the kale to the oven and bake for a further 5 minutes.

CREAMY KALE AND BROAD BEAN STEW

This light summer stew can be served as a main meal or as a side dish. Its
creamy sauce pairs well with champ or new potatoes.
This recipe also works well with chard.

275g/10oz kale leaves
4 tablespoons olive oil
1 red onion, diced
2 garlic cloves, finely chopped
2 leeks, trimmed, washed and sliced
3 celery stalks, diced
a medium glass of white wine
275g/10oz fresh or frozen
 podded broad beans

300ml/1¼ cups vegetable stock
2 bay leaves
a few sprigs of thyme
150ml/⅔ cup double cream
1 teaspoon grainy mustard
a handful of tarragon leaves
salt and black pepper

Strip the kale leaves from their central stem and thinly slice. Blanch the prepared
kale for a couple of minutes and refresh with cold water.

Heat the olive oil in a heavy-bottomed pan, stir in the onion, garlic, leeks
and celery, cover the pan and sweat the vegetables until they start to soften
but not brown.

Pour in the wine, bring to the boil and keep at a fast boil until it has reduced
by half. Add the podded beans, stock and bay leaves, cover the pan and simmer
for 5 minutes.

Add the blanched kale, cream, mustard and tarragon, season to taste and
gently simmer for a further 5 minutes. Remove the bay leaves before serving.